High Poets Society

Society

— II —

by

b. abbott

Monarch Publishing, 2018
www.monarchbookstore.com

———

Poem on page 20 was first published by *The Boston Globe* in April 2016.

Poem on page 24 was first published by *Your One Phone Call* in June 2016.

You're in the stars, you're in the breeze;
    not just only in our memories.
We'll forget you not,
        your love lives on.
Even if your
        presence is gone.
                    - For Leah

greatest hits - side a

b. abbott

You're wrong for me
but I'm alright with that.

Even if broken and defeated,
I still love all your pi e ce s.

Hell isn't; being alone.
It's more like calling
      someone else's
arms home.

I hate that our
h e a r t s
are this far
a p a r t .

Her
mind
was
lost
in
thoughts
of plots;
escaping
reality
at whatever
the

cost.

b. abbott

You're the piece of me
which brings me peace.

I'm loving,
I'm grateful,
I stimulate your mind
and I'll kill any motherfucker
who doubts you are mine.

b. abbott

I want the parts which
you keep to yourself;
all the secrets,
you've told no one else.

She asked me why I was so good to her
and that question mark at the end of that sentence

made me feel like every guy in the past
treated her the exact opposite as she deserved.

I cannot speak as fast as I think, missing words and perfection as I stumble to get it all out.

I have just so very much to say to you and it plays out in my head so perfectly but as soon as I begin to talk I stutter and you've caught me.

I cannot hide now, you know me too well and already know what I was about to say.

Shine on, motherfucker.
Don't ever let them,
ever dim your bright.

Someone's always trying to steal my light.
And I'm like,
"Nah, motherfucker. You can't burn this bright."

When I met you I realized
love was a feeling I hadn't felt before
and now that I know how it feels,
it's a feeling I can't ignore.

b. abbott

You colored my heart
but you didn't stay inside the lines.
And when I asked why,
you replied, "Love is blind."

Give me one excuse why you won't take that risk.
Why you won't lean in a little closer and steal that kiss.
Life's too short to ever resist
      a love so real it makes you feel it exist.

It's not as if tomorrow's ever promised,
so feel free to kiss me anytime,
grab my hand or pull me close,
to remind me, you are mine.

Our souls are connected
our hearts are too;
long before
there was a me and you.

On top of flannel sheets,
where our feet do meet;
a place of war and peace.

Peculiar feelings seem to exist,
after all these years
butterflies seem to persist.

fromage

b. abbott

We are created with two eyes,
two arms, two legs but one heart;
just so we can find the soul
whose chest possesses its counterpart.

Make me think.
Make me laugh.
Make my heart beat twice as fast.
Make me always check if you're looking back.
    And my soul will be all yours to have.

It will always be me and you.
Always ride or die.
No matter the direction we are going;
always side-by-side.

You found
  your way
into my
    comfort zone
and now
I never
want
to be in
there
alone.

It's in those moments
when you're next to me
and my lungs,
somehow,
forget to breathe
and I can't think straight,
I'm a mess it seems,
that I'm grateful they came true;
all of my dreams.

Notice the glowing on my face.
It's caused by you,
as if you're
the Sun's rays.

The best mornings
    are the ones
which start at noon,
    but I awake at eight
        to lay in bed with you.

We are two souls intertwined;
I'm part of yours and you're part of mine.

It feels so good to say it,
even better to hear it said.
I love you.
I love you.
I love you.
over
and over,
again.

No matter how old my bones
may become,
your love
makes my soul feel young.

Little parts of you exist in
       my being,
         my soul,
             my heart
             and all the fibers in between.

It's as if your heartbeat shaped this heart of mine
and like any good artist you took your time,
slowly sculpting every line
and always staying within the design.

The moments I wish
lasted forever,
always seemed to be
the ones you and I
were together.

The part when our lives intertwined;
That will forever be a favorite of mine.

muerte

b. abbott

Last night I saw a girl,
who looked just like you.
She noticed me staring.
She felt it too.
She saw the look in my eyes.
As I imagined you there.
I just couldn't help it.
I just had to stare.
She looked back, confused.
As she sat with her date.
I couldn't even eat,
left the food on my plate.
I kept looking back,
lost in our world, in my brain.
A feeling so strong,
she wondered, why she felt the same.
It poured out my eyes,
from the depths of my soul.
I started to burn up.
But outside was so cold.
The feeling persists,
for the rest of the night.
I look back as I leave;
maybe it's you, this time..
Disappointment again.
For she is not you.
And if you were her,
I'd barely be able to move.
Frozen in time,
I can't move my feet
I don't know what I'd do,
if we ever did meet.

Like a masterpiece
hanging on the wall.
Some people walk by it
but I stand in awe.
I see the true meaning,
to me it just calls.
It pulls me in gently
but quickly I fall.
Brushstrokes so simple,
but like nothing I ever saw.
So photo realistic;
to it, I am drawn.
The gallery becomes empty,
all but me have gone.
I stand there staring
for hours past dawn.
Once my eyes leave it
I start to have withdrawals.
I can't look away
for fear I won't recall.

A smile that's contagious
and lips with that flavor.
I thank God he made her.
A perfect cut with his razor.

She turns the negative into Sunshine.
And I fell in love with her rays.

The chaos is
loud but I don't
know how to
love any other
way.

Today is yesterday's tomorrow, while tomorrow is the day after's past.
I want to be with you forever, our love will surely last.

I could never imagine
being anyone else.
They don't have you.
They are living in Hell.

I don't know where you are. Its dinnertime, you are late.
You don't pick up your phone,
and my heart starts to race.
I wonder what is wrong and my stomach starts to ache.
The only remedy is when I hear you
turn the key to our place.
Dinners all ready, food-getting cold on the plate,
I am not hungry, I cannot eat.
I just yearn for your taste.
I am going crazy.
I don't know how much more I can take.
And all I can think is that I pray you are safe.
Thoughts running through my mind
as I sit and contemplate.
What should be done, what moves should I make
The feeling burns deep, the unknowing, I just hate.
There's nothing I can do, just have to leave it all to fate.
Then you walk through the door.
I see the glow on your face.
My heart skips a beat, like we are on our first date.
I see it in your eyes that you can hardly wait.
You have something to tell me,
you don't know exactly what to say.
We waited for this moment, since our wedding day.
You say that you are pregnant
and I get to pass on my last name.

She shimmers, she shines.
　　　She's a constellation I call mine.

Walking 'round Boston.
Holding hands in the Common.
I whisper; I love you…. incase you've forgotten.
A feeling not foreign,
of love that has blossomed.
Call it Springtime or opposite of Autumn.
A feeling that's awesome,
and won't soon be forgotten.
I'll remember this day and recall it often.

We are walking down the street.
Walking arm in arm.
Walk past an old lady,
"You two are so in love."
She sees it in our eyes.
The way you hold my hand.
It's just our first date,
but forever I'm your man.

I used to hold my breath, when I was a kid, every time
we drove through a tunnel.
Sometimes in traffic I didn't think I'd make it out
the other end without passing out.
Now, since you've left,
I've been holding my breath
and I don't think I'll ever breathe again.

Waiting forever is less
      heartbreaking than loving another.

Oh most gracious virgin Mary
You didn't answer my prayers
You left me weeping weeping weeping
You didn't even hear
Like you didn't even care
You left me weeping weeping weeping
Sitting on the stairs
Wiping away the tears
Weeping weeping weeping
Like you didn't even care
Like you didn't even care.

Such a dreary, wet winter week,
I hear crows crawl closer as we speak.
I lay lifeless learning of my demise,
as her heart helps me close my eyes.

Every time you fall asleep, you wake up as someone else.
The only thing you can prove is consciousness of self.
Memories so real, as if you can't even tell
that before you fell asleep, you were living
in a different Hell.

I live

In a world

In my

Own mind.

It's different than those

Who live

On

The outside.

b. abbott

e.e.

b. abbott

To you I should be microscopic(lintinyourpocket)
but for some reason
loves defies logic(,scienceandprophets)

You belong here but in no particular place.
As long as it's nexttome and we're sharingthesamespace.

You're close to perfection,
but even if not,
I'd seek your affection,
until feelings were caught.

She's emotional. A girl with a bunch of soul. Crying over characters which are fictional, people she doesn't know, and the occasional stray animal and I love how she wastes time watching flowers grow... how could you ask fo(r) mo(re)?

There's not a spot on the map,
where I wouldn't come from,
if you needed my back(ing),
front or side
soul or mind,
wherever you are
whatever the time.

b. abbott

You made things so darn easy;
opening up,
falling in love,
perfecting my touch,
 all of the above.

(like you didn't even mean to)

I said "I love you.",
then cowered
ssslllooowwwlllyyy;
waiting for the
weight of the world to
come
crashing
d
o
w
n
.

But as I braced for impact
I was greeted
with a
flood of relief,
just as your lips
p a r t e d
and you
said it back.

Lunchbox love notes.
Homemade cards.
When you touch my arm,
or my leg in the car.
Out-of-the-blue text, emails, or, calls.
That look. Especially that look.
When you bite your lip,
when you run your fingers through my hair,
when you get so close I can't move
and don't want to(or it, to ever end).
Bad songs only you think are good
but I end up liking because you do.
The recipes that never come out just right but the effort fills my soul
and empty stomach.

All the times I've died a little, I've kept living for those things.

I'm constantly reminded
of things I cannot
see.
I'm constantly reminded
of the love you have
for me.
I'm constantly reminded
of what is yet
to be.
I'm constantly reminded
you and I are now
We.

I dream to leave this all behind.
Where I don't need money, love will do just fine.
There will be me and you to pass the time.
We'll watch the leaves change and slowly die.
Till we (you and I) part ways with our last goodbye.

The more (i think)
The more (it's love)
The more (i do)
The more (i fuck up).

My reflection in the pond
looks so alone
since you've gone
and the trees,
standing together behind me,
can't help but look so lone-el-lee (lonely).

Somewhere amongst the daffodils,
I remembered your scent as if you were still
here
or there
or everywhere
and even if not
your essence will
(be).

Death walked over me and right on by and the apple tree in my grand-pa's yard is now at least ten feet high. I'm still going, growing under the Sun's shine but the fruit doesn't taste just as sweet as in the days when you were mine.

I sit here wondering what it's like basking in your Sun.
What your Moon is like on the planet where you're from? How many
hours are in the day once an orbit has begun? And if there are pretty
flowers there which remind you of someone?

(Me.)

b. abbott

still no light

b. abbott

I believe in the Earth,
in the pain I cause,
in the pain I feel,
in the fire,
the love,
which burns in my
soul,
my gut,
my whole.
I go on
towards love,
towards fear,
through anything standing
in front of me,
in between
you and I.

I followed this path. Through forest, through mud, over rocks and
fallen trees. It crossed rivers under stars as I walked the valleys. And
as I emerged there was this drawbridge in front of me and I knew I'd
fall in love on the other side, where I could see. There you were as it
descended slowly. And as I crossed into a garden of happy, the flowers
blossomed and the Sun shined brightly.

I push the limits
just to feel loved,
wanted,
obsessed over,
all of the above.

A sledgehammer across the chest sent shivers down my spine. As if I've known you a thousand years but it was seeing you for the first time.

Am I the only one whose world it is you
       shake? For I can't tell the difference;
when I'm lost within your quakes.

I love just how you see the world and imagine things I'd never dream. Your perspective is beautiful and allowing me to glance through your lenses is a pleasure. I sink when you swim, fall when you fly and that is why I love seeing the world through your eyes.

hps — ll —

I'd burn in Dante's fire,
I'd drown in Melville's sea;
I'd never read a book again,
 if it meant you loving me.

b. abbott

You're an abstract
work of art,
who contemporarily
completes
my
modern heart.

You're not just a reason to wake up.
You have me jumping so high out of bed
I could win a gold medal.
I'm ready to start the day with you
before my eyes even crack open.
No snooze button.
No 15 more minutes.
I literally cannot wait to see your face again.
Now if only this dream would end...

Bombs drop in the fields,
on the beaches,
the dunes,
the sand,
the mud of my heart.
They destroy the strings
which keep the muscles
of my love
on the proper coordinates.
The frequency
of the collisions
shake my core,
my soul,
my all.
But in the destruction
love stands
victorious,
triumphant,
in jubilee
in spite
of all efforts
to strike
it down.

Gently welcoming love is how it came to be.
As if you floated gracefully down, instead of
falling in love with me.

b. abbott

I love the early morning birds,
who sing songs
which I never heard,
in Sunlight not often observed
and all I can think is how that is absurd.

"Heartbreak and other lies";
should be the title to my life.

I punch myself in the gut.
And yell the words, "toughen up!"
There are no cowards in the game of love.
It kills those that aren't strong as fuck.

Ninety percent of not wanting to sleep
is shutting off the light so me
and the darkness can meet.

I'm having trouble with anxiety,
    it's replaced all the love inside of me.

I drown in your depths.
But yet,
there is no regret
within my last breath.

As if everything is new and everything is old.
I've felt this before.
I've felt us before, it seems and through some tear in space and time
here we are again; strangers.
But your eyes look so damn familiar.
I can't be wrong. I've felt this before.
In another body with a different heart,
but someway, somehow my soul remembers this part...

How do you expect to roar with lions
when all you've done is purr at cats?

I'm everything you want to be
but nothing you'll become.
You're second place,
you lost the race
and I'm still champion.

I'm nice not weak,
there's a difference in between.
So watch where you sleep;
I'm a nightmare not a dream.

I believe in peace,
even if it's unrealistic.
I feel
it in me,
in this world that is twisted.

I do not understand the people without ambition.
The non-dreamers, the ones without three wishes.
The ones who go to work just to make a living,
with no love, no passion, no heart given.

I live for those
"I love this song",
"So, I met this girl",
"You are never gonna
believe what happened",
"I swear on my mother's life",
"Just trust me",
"Close your eyes",
moth-er-fuck-ing
moments.
The rest is filler, time I will never get back. Fluff.
It's those moments I'll always cherish;
the good stuff.

microdots

b. abbott

You are
 the soul
to my mate
and all
 the rest
 were just
 fakes.

Why did I fall in love?
Oh yeah,
     because I'm dumb.

What's worse;
never getting
what you need
or constantly
worrying that
it'll leave?

Were we friends,
family, lovers
or more?
All I know,
is my soul
has met
yours before.

Utterly in love with what we'll
become.

To whomever
falls in love with me;
I wish you luck,
genuinely.

To be in love with you,
        is to be the luckiest fool.

This is where we differ slightly;
I'm in love
and
you
just
like
me.

Something about
my personal space
 that I don't mind
if you invade.

Some people just touch
your skin,
while others touch
something,
you hold within.

She hates being told she's perfect;
    for she only sees the fucked up version.

She grew wings and learned to fly
because they said she couldn't, if she tried.

Please, never let me go.
> I'll stay forever, if you'd just say so.

b. abbott

Our hands are like magnets;
        always attracted.

Let's skip the lifetimes
which
we
aren't
together.

It's this deep,
      dark love which I crave....
not easily found
 and more
      rarely obtained.

I'm obsessed with being part of your life.
I want forever but I'd settle for a night.

I'm needy, I'm attached;
I need to know you love me back.

I wouldn't even use the next 2 wishes;
the one on you would be sufficient.

I wanted to smile so I looked at a picture of you.

I think about you so much;
I feel more you than me.

I have
more
than I'll
ever need,
at any time
because
you love me.

I
don't
fall
in love
with
people
      I see;
I
fall
in love
 with
souls
      I meet.

I deserve
your best
but I still love your mess.

I always
thought
love was
a myth
then I
met you
and found
out it exists.

How many times have our souls met?
And how many more, until it's perfect?

Four letters;
keep us
together.

Every second which you wait,
        is another towards too late.

All this mayhem and
I still choose you.

A vibe
 which
was
magic
and she
 knew
she had it.

A second spent with you
    is better than eternity with someone new.

weather or not

b. abbott

"He loves me." "He loves me not."
Pick another flower in case you forgot.
And as the petals blow in the wind,
release all the memories you had of him.

A single raindrop doesn't ruin a whole day
but it's always the start of torrential rain.

I'm ready to come in; it's raining here, outside.
So just open the door; stop this storm, which I cry.

If your hand was nowhere to be found
as I clawed my way up from the ground
don't expect to see my hand reach out,
as I float over you, on my cloud.

It's how the Sun's rays paint your skin
and the way I'm left in awe till the clouds roll in.

Just another cloudy night and I cannot see the Moon.
So instead, I close my eyes and try to dream of you.

My ice caps melt,
August feels like June.
I can only explain this,
as my globe being warmed by you.

One little drop of rain
and out of nowhere the flooding came.
The tides grew rough,
the current was strong
but this good cry is what my soul needed all along.

The thunder outside is insane
    but doesn't compare to the storm in my brain.

There will always be some cloudy days;
thunder, lightening, even rain.
But I promise that if you remain;
my Sun will somehow shine again.

You can wait for rain and chase down clouds
or you can try to enjoy the Sunshine here right now.

She wears shades of blue....
   An attempt to brighten up
      the darkness which surrounds her.

In my half awake, half asleep state
that I find myself in every morning,
you're all that is running through my mind.
As my body is paralyzed and my heart is racing,
in that moment I am happiest; for we are together.
But once I'm jolted awake,
reality interrupts that heaven and
I open my eyes
to hell in disguise
as bright blue, shining skies.

modern love

I think I fell in love today
while scrolling somewhere on your page.
You're such a beautiful stranger;
              I can't wait to know
and find out if your pictures match your soul.

Look up from your palms and into my eyes;
the second you take will be worth the time.

I'm the phone,
you're wifi at home
and we connect as if the password is known.

I ignore all the texts,
all the likes and friend requests
and that's how I know I'm in love with you.

Text me all day,
fuck me all night
and we'll be good
for the rest of our lives.

Even after we say goodnight,
I still check for that notification light.

I text most people
then forget
what I said
but when I text you,
I count the seconds
till it's read.

I don't care
if anyone
texts me again,
all because
I lost
my best friend.

I just realized how much I missed you.
Something important happened to me today
and my animal instincts had me reaching for my phone
but as that signal traveled from my brain,
through my arm to my thumb, to make that call;
I realized I wasn't able to do that.

You text "hello" and I don't know; if I should reply with "hi" or maybe "why?"

No matter how many times my phone rings,
I think it's you and my heart, sinks.

I stay awake till 4 a.m.
    just in case you call, again.

The light blinks and I think it's her.
The screen is black so I'm unsure.
I swipe to see if it is true.
I've been l waiting all day for a text from you.

I've been waiting for this text
but too scared to read what it says.

I logged on and checked your page,
just like any other day.
You posted pictures, they were new.
And when I saw, it was clear we were through.

I wanted to hear your voice so bad;

                                                     I craved it.

So, I listened to the voice mail I had;

                                                     I saved it.

So many things,
I wish I never said.
So many times,
I wish I never pressed send...

B. Abbott, the Boston-based writer, whose poems have been featured in the *Boston Globe*, *Your One Phone Call*, *Scarlet Leaf Review* and many other online publications, has found his stronghold in the world of social media with 250k+ followers under the moniker of @HighPoetsSociety. His debut publication *High Poets Society* is an Amazon bestseller and can be found at Barnes and Noble nationwide.

INSTAGRAM
@highpoetssociety

FACEBOOK
HighPoetsSociety

WEBSITE
www.highpoetssociety.com

High Poets Society

by B. Abbott

This is Brian Abbott's first major publication.
The Boston-based writer has found his stronghold in the world of
social media under the moniker of High Poets Society. His writing is most
recognized for it's mesmerizing rhyme scheme and clever wordplay.

a

silver

tongue

with

iron

lungs

CPSIA information can be obtained
at www.ICGtesting.com
Printed in the USA
BVOW09s2134150418
513468BV00017B/389/P

9 781945 322099